The poems found in the following pages represent the culmination of twenty years of poetry writing. I began writing poetry long before that, of course, but most of it is lost.

Some of the poems are reflective, some happy, many looking at internal pain and strife – the rich vein without which many poets would struggle to find a subject!

Over the years I have, like everyone else, had relationships the nature of which I did not begin to understand until long afterwards. Very much a case of "if I'd only known then what I know now". I hope that because we've all got these emotions in common you will find at least one of the poems in this book that resonates with you long after you have read it.

I would like to thank my friends especially Susi and David and Carole, my family particularly my children – ever supportive! – my parents and last but by no means least, my beloved husband Jim, without whom life would have little meaning and very little colour.

MUSINGS OF A LOST SOUL

a journey without end

RUTH WOOD

ISBN: 978-1-4092-5132-3

(c) 2009

a poem for

james

*J*ust when I thought I would never find
love

*A*nd life would be empty and grey

*M*ourning the time spent below not
above

*E*ach endless, meaningless day.

*S*uddenly your kiss awoke my sad life

*W*aking my slumbering heart

*O*pening up a new way as your wife

*O*rdering each fragile part

*D*eepening love's tender dart.

ALONE IN THAME

I stand
naked
in my hotel room.

look at me
I shout
silently

am I not worth
a second glance?

I know my waist
Is larger
than before
and my hips
have spread
to Wales -

But look beyond!
See the uncharted
parts
of my mind.

I can waltz with you
until sunrise
or talk of Wolf
and Sondheim.

I can pass on knowledge
that will open doors
and let you fly
free.

So –

LOOK AT ME!

BAT YAM

ISRAEL 29/3/01

The bright sounds of the city reach up through
holy skies
and round the open window where I lie.
This ancient land of secrets where Christ and
Moses walked
has found my aching soul where troubles die.

I dream of angels waking with eyes of glowing fire
who breathe their hope upon this warring land.
Their wing tips softly touching, they speak to me of
love
but not in ways that I can understand.

For all that life is precious, and death is but a
pause,
the echoes of the messengers will fade.
This place of souls=redemption will never be at
peace
while Mammon rules the God that man has made.

First published "With hearts ablaze" 2003

CAROL ANN

Today I met a poet
a real weaver of words
who has seen more life
than I can even imagine.

She is strong
and dark
and very convincing.

So why do I find her words
less than right?
Not moving
or even loving.

I must have so shallow a thought
that I do not see
her depths.
The dimensions she brings
to you and I
are lost
in my ears.

Yet to talk to her
is light and meaning
and friendship not missed
until found.
A fertile ground
for such as I.

So much more to learn
to be
and to see
before I can aspire to call myself
the start
of a poet.

Champagne at night – hidden!

The cork from my
small
bottle of champagne
has just hit
my bedroom ceiling.

So much for stealth.

The smell – as the champagne
flows
out of the bottle
is filling the room
as obvious
as stale sex
or cheap perfume.

The sound – as the cork left the bottle –
seemed
so loud it could not be missed.

But you appear
not to have heard.

So I can still lie
in my lonely bed
drink champagne
eat chocolates
and dream of a blue-eyed lover
who can make the world
fizz.

Like my once-discreet
bottle of champagne.

First published "Forever Spoken" 2007

COLOURS FOR YOU

I want to tell you
how the sun shines when I think of you,
how the rainbow lingers when I talk of you,
how the tide stops when I long for you.

I want to show you
how my skin glows when I feel of you
how my eyes shine when I try for you
how my hands reach when I long for you.

I want to sing you
when the chord sounds that is there for you
when the note peals that is meant for you
when the time beats that is struck for you.

My whole life
waits in the dark for you
holds its breath still for you
colours all the seas for you.

My death now will
only stop time for you
Dream richly anew for you
break all my cells for you.

I know that my world is you
blue and red for you
green and black for you
life and death for you.

My arms motion here for you
in the light for you
in the dark for you

Help me find my world with you.

DEDICATION

I'm in a land of dark despair
where fetid swamps corrupt
the air;
No hope of help, or thought of
life,
Jut hopelessness and constant
strife.

The darkness comes to cover
me
I shut my eyes so I can't see.
My mind screams out for
someone who
can bring me help, can see me
through.

You heard my cry in silence
sent
and answered my
bewilderment.
I gave my trust, You held me
fast,
and showed me how this peace
could last.

DEMONS AND NIGHT FEARS

The clock ticks its course through the hours at its
station,
it's old fettered face has turned blank in the night,
while hands that are weary with no destination
sweep slowly to dawn and the filtering light.

I lie in my bed as the wind howls and shatters
the branches of oak trees who do not resist.
My feeling of loneliness no longer matters,
whilst demons and night fears soon cease to exist.

Don't turn to the past with its cargo of laughter,
where mirth was the bond and good feelings held
sway.
It wasn't the truth that rang out to the rafters
and held every happy thought burnt in its clay.

But rather look through to the next golden season.
Calmly wait out the incredible tide.
Love is still here beyond hope and all reason,
Fate's law has decreed I belong at your side.

Third prize winner

"Best poems and Poets" 2002

FIND THE LIGHT

See your scene
and find the light
so clear, so true.
My scene is fixed
the light is not
your eyes see through.

I move so close
we touch and hold
in wonder spelled.
This cannot be
it is untrue
our colours meld.

For both a first
a new idea
that holds us fast.
With such ideals
we had, we lose
yet this will last.

In mind's vast world
in secret signs
we hold our own.
Your wisdom calls
my mind replies
our souls are one.

2004

<u>For M e</u>

You are complete
and I envy that.
You have no understanding
of my empty state.

I am pleased that you have
such joy
at the heart of all you are.

For a while I touched it.

But now, for me
there can be no firm centre
no strong family tie
no love of life.

I know I can give much
of what I am
tn my chosen tasks;.

But deep inside,
where it matters
I see no-one.

I was born alono

and so

will I die .

GREEN PATCH OF THISTLES

Just watch in silent loneness
while he speaks.

Nod your head — make approving
noises
he'll not know.

Not know that in your heart
there is no sound.

Just keep the solemn silence
in the wilderness
the green patch of thistles
that used to be
your heart.

Just learn that in life
there are no new beginnings.

Nothing changes.

You have never been on board
the train of exclusivity.
You have always stood beside the tracks
of loneliness and abhorrence.

Learn this lesson well

it will only come again.

Heart

The heart you gave me
nestles
in the hollow
of my throat
where you kissed me.

And my pulse races.

I lie in my bed
amid the wreckage
of newspapers
and beer
and ponder on the life
I've led

Until now.

What strange
and twisting
path
has brought me through
the wilderness
of broken dreams
the desert of all hope
and brought me here.

I have two ways to go

Either I see you as unprofessional
A flawed man
Who cannot do his job

Or

I see you as a flawed human
Like me

With worries and troubles
that overwhelm

So

which way do I go.

You are supposed to
show me the way

You are
the knowledgeable man
who can cure me.

I have put my hope in you
so where
do I go

Which way
cast
my vote.

JERICHO

It was a short walk to Jericho
to hear the trumpets sound;
to see the soldiers of the Lord,
the scavengers,
take control.

We marched across the plains
until we reached the walls;
then round went the soldiers of the Lord
blowing conch shells,
sounding trumpets.

And the people who lived in the city –
what of them? What of those shining ones
who did not know the soldiers of the Lord
just the war
and the trouble?

We went peacefully on our way to Jericho,
but the others had gone before us.
And those that became the soldiers of the Lord
drank the wine
and celebrated.

I KNOW SO

Is it wrong to know
you love me?
Does it take you for granted
to feel
your caring with me
always.
When we are away from each other's sight
do you feel me
as I feel you?
I know so.

Does it worry you to know
how much I care?
Will you think at night
when I'm not there
that I am thinking of you
and feeling you
close?
I know so.

Can this love between us
this certain life
continue in the calm, cold
light of day?
Or, a victim of the dying shadows
of dreams once held
now gone away
Fade, like the ghosts
of summer past
into the mist
and dying sun?
I know not.

Once held, a warmth is always there
once said, God will always hold a prayer
Once felt, our love will always share
I know so.

June 2003

LAST POEM

Once he cared.

Before the other things caught up
and life became hard
and ugly.

He had enough love to share
to want the best for me
before the world caught up
before the DVT,

He loves me still - he says -
as much as he can do.
I think it may be true.

But life has held its cast
and all that love is past.

And I am too.

October 2001

KNOW ME

If there is no despair in your soul
you do not know me.

If your steps are firm and full of strength
you cannot help.

To see what I need is to understand
the black and lonely fields of night,
the lion runs, and tiger haunts
and deadly paths of dreams.

The nightmare world of my life
cannot accept your voice.
Your look does not exist
within this rotten, tarnished wood.

No matter how you try to reach the
essence
Me
there is no road that takes you
safely through.

My way is thorns and black demonic
knife
And soon I'll end my dark and brooding
life.

LEANING DOWN THE STAIRS

It was a moment born of wonder
in a world of noise
and movement.

We stood still
of necessity.
The pose was such
that each upon each
the stairs had their fill.

I don't recall who was above
because, as I turned
and looked down,
I was caught in the web
of the golden eyes.
And the depth of ages
thrilled and held me
mute and trembling.

I knew every part of my skin
that touched yours.
My body settled so cxactly
knowing each contour
feeling your force.

Without moving
you drew me into your self
and I was glad to go.

I could have stayed
silent,
frozen
in time and light
until all the unseen stars winked out
one by one.

But such is life that all
had to break
and the pieces fell one
into another
and we moved.

And afterward
I wished I'd leaned a little more
down the stairs.

December 2001

<u>M ARK WELL</u>

The greatest and most worthy love
Born of need, formed by thought, kept by
time
Is not of ordinary kind
Found by common mortals in the sand.

Touched by God its prayer is strong, true,
kind
Looking outward, sharing much
and understanding all.

Echoes of the present mind
will only strengthen and confirm
not hinder.

Its growing form sustained by tenderness
As each is nurtured
within its strong centre
will hold all floating hopes
and shape the hears
of all Its hosts.

Keep well this love if it should deign to call,
for having once tasted of the crystal wine
it will not come again.

MOTORWAY MEANING

Each finger has its own
memory
of touch
and smoothly gliding
promise.

The nails are quick to give
response
to the firm hold;

then, slowly caressing
the warmth feels along
each side
and returns
the same way.

Every nerve is waking
warming
flaming
sending shivers of sheer pleasure
to other centres
as yet
untouched.

MUSINGS OF A LOST SOUL

I feel ......

distanced

apart

alone

Again

after all life=s tumult

all that has happened.

After tasting happiness -

that illusory word.

Thinking ⱭI am home@.

The welcome mat has been pulled

from under my feet.

No doubt for washing.

But the mud of disillusion

sticks

for a long long time.

MY GARDEN

There are weeds in my
borders
where once there were
flowers,
they are creeping up in me
and changing the hours.

The roses are fading
their colours are gone
the shadows grow longer
where once bright sun shone.

The paths in my garden
have crumbled to dust
their edges are blurring
in dirt and disgust.

How long can I wander
and watch the decay?
My garden has weeds and
is fading away.

NO COMPLICATIONS!

No complications
would seem to be the order of the night

and in the darkened
bathroom-lit
bed
it seemed reasonable.

It seemed it was understood
what complications meant.
No wining or dining
no public admission
of private excess.

Once this would have been the cause
of breast-beating
of constant analysis
of dramatic crying in the night.

But now -
no complications
is exactly what it says.
And still seems
reasonable.

NO TOUCH

No touch today
a laugh
a smile
But no caress.

A move away
a look
a sigh
And – something less.

You still feel kind
a friend
a pal
But nothing more

I'll hold my mind
a day
a year
Though not restore.

No touch today
a space
a sigh
The closeness gone.

Then go away
go past
go now
I stand alone.

QUESTIONS OF GHENT

When we go to Ghent
will you feel you're strong enough
to offer what I need?

When we are in Ghent
will your story tell the tale
to help my longings feed?

When we stay in Ghent
will your feelings match the thought
and open up my life?

When we come from Ghent
will it all have been worthwhile
to keep it from your wife?

so why am I crying

So why am I crying?
When everything is perfect
and the man of my dreams is here.

and why am I crying
when I know this is the Eden
I've been waiting to appear

Yes, why am I crying?
If everything is perfect
and I've made the change I want

So why am I crying?
Is it the wine
that's filled me with tears from
nowhere.

So why am I crying?
Please – someone – tell me?

STRANGE POETRY

I breathed
    a prayer
And sent it winging
    up

        up
then waited to see
    if it had been
        heard.
Then
    after a while
        as I waited
I felt
    guided
        comforted
            helped

and knew that my prayer
    would be
        answered.
So I allowed
    my life
        to just
            happen
As it would
    alone for me
and you appeared.

I would never
    in a thousand years
        of guessing
arrive
    at this
        solution.

A completely new
    and unique
        experience
for both of us.

THANKS ED!

"How do you feel?"

Yes – how do I feel?
This is just a question I can answer.

"You know how you feel"

I <u>know</u> how I feel!
I am at the ending of the process.

"Where will you go?"

Yes – where <u>will</u> I go?
I'll go to the future that is owed me.

"Will you be well?"

I know I'll be well.
Now I am in control of my progress.
The past will never harm me
Now I hold the key entirely.

Thanks Ed!

THE CHANGE?

My writing has changed.
How strange.

It has been, at times various
large, small
looping, cramped
flowing or stilted.

It has crept upwards across the page
and downwards towards itself.

It has been good, and bad
and unreadable.

But now
it remains consistent
for more than two lines together.

It is small, but contained,
neat and immediately clear.
Comprehensible in its black meanings
across the straight edged page.

Does this show how I, too, have changed?
From the incomprehensible
flowing in different directions at once,
getting nowhere
and unreadable
to a calm, confident smooth and contained
flowing.

THE HARDEST POEM TO WRITE

So now I sit and ponder
on the power I seem to wield
not aware of its existence
'til today;
I would never want to hurt you
or to cause your life to change
I care too much about you
to betray.

I thought that by not saying
what I knew my heart had sung
you wouldn't see the truth of
my mind's glow;
but you saw it all in spite
of my efforts not to speak.
I know I made it hard for
you to go.

I understand your reasons
and I love you all the more
for standing by your purpose
and your life.
All that which goes to make you
the warm person that you are
is rightly not for me but
for your wife.

But maybe just a little
of the man I've learned to trust
can lodge within my heart and
in my soul.
You've taught me about feelings
and the things I didn't know
your caring shows, and helps to
make me whole.

the hours of the night

Are you sleeping, my love,
in your bed that we shared
are you turning to reach for my
shade?
Are you lonely and thinking
of times that we kissed
are you happy, or are you
afraid?

I want to be with you
all the hours of the night
every minute of each passing
day.
This feeling of longing
that fills me inside
is a pain that will not go away.

Tomorrow I'll see you
and kiss your sweet mouth,
your arms will fold round me
and hold.
The rest of the world
will fade out as we touch
and love's warmth will soon
banish the cold.

THIEF*!*

He looked like anyone –

someone's son
someone's love
someone's hope
someone's joy –

just another normal boy.

He came to church –

came to pray
came to look
came to think
came to hope
came to ask –

just another visitor.

And then he went –

went with black
went with dark
went with tears
went with hurt
went with Satan –

just another burglar.

October 2001

OUR FATHER IN HEAVEN

Our father in heaven hallowed be your name
In worship we follow on earth just the same
Your kingdom is coming through Jesus your son
For mankind all will love you and your will be
done.

On this day oh feed us with your daily bread,
With love and with honour your children are fed
And though we are sinning forgive all our woes
As we see our brethren as friends not as foes.

And when we fall down Lord, through dark velvet
night
Then take us from evil and lead to your light
For yours is the power, the glory and might
We follow you always and stay in your sight.

THE PSYCHOLOGIST

I know the pattern of this carpet well –
the colour
the texture
the ingrained fears.

This is what I study
when I feel your calm gaze resting heavily
upon me.

You wait in professional silence
with a patience acquired down the years
knowing I must eventually
speak.

Some days I can barely sit still –
my foot tapping
my mind's frantic whisperings.

But –

You see it all
and store it up
ready to write on the blue lines
in the manilla folder of my life.

It will all come round to me in time.

Today I am not sure why I came.
My original wishes hard-changed
and the churning desires inside
coalesced
into rock
certainty.

All my life I have longed for a peace

that would come
when I am whole.

But –

now you are taking all those pieces
and patiently weaving them
together
with blanket stitches.

I cannot trust it.
I dare not trust you.

You are doing your job
you are paid for your sympathy
and I cannot take that one leap of faith.

For
very soon now
you,too,
as all the others,
will move on
and pass me back
like a small bundle of dirty washing
to whoever follows on.

The defences I have built in my needful life
cannot be dismantled in
a day
a month
a year.

For –

when they are gone
and the barriers are down

how will I defend against the night?

Protect myself against the day?

Keep away from the fire?

And recognise the Devil
when he finally comes to call.

But –
still –

I need your help.

21/3/02

I thought this time
it's right
you loved me – as me
and all that I am.

But I am unlovable
This I now know.

When you thought you knew me
you loved me
But now

How can love survive when I cannot
live up
to what you want?

I love you more than I have loved
anyone.

But it is not enough.

You need someone who can know how
to love you
who can be what you want.

I don't think it's me.

I was born to disappoint
And I am fulfilling my destiny.

I don't know what to do
Because I love you so much
it hurts.

THE TRAMP

He was an old man
bent and shufflingly grey.
He looked out on his sad kingdom
through pale, rheumy eyes.

No-one knew how old he was –
he could not tell, he had lost count.
Where he had lived, and how,
were misty and unknown
even by him.

His world had shrunk with his frame
until now his hope
was encompassed by five large carrier bags
which he kept, neatly stored.
Each day he walked the streets
his eyes on the cracked flags
his ears unaware.
The world did not care.

One night, alone, dark,
evil came.
He was left sad and bleeding
but alive.
And resigned to the kicks and the blows
he had not invited.

And the people around felt shame/
He had lived among them
but not quite belonging/
And now his familiar figure had gone
driven away by mindless vandals.
We miss him.

November 2000

<u>TO JIM : MY PERFECT ONE</u>

For each of us there is a soul
outside the common run
another spirit like our own
the matching, perfect one.

For each of us God draws a plan
and sketches in our life
then puts in place the perfect one
as husband or as wife.

For both of us there came a time
when what was meant came true
our souls met, found the perfect one
my perfect one – is you.

Why does my heart ache
for a man I scarcely know?
Why do I long to hear his deep voice say
Ahello@
What is this power
that sets my skin on fire?
How to explain it
this wishing, this desire.

What can I do now
to keep this flame alight,
Why do I waken in the middle
of the night?
Why do my dreams flow
with images of death
flowing like rivers on one last
lingering death.

How will I know if
he feels the heat of time
Do I still want him to know

WHERE AM I NOW?

It was
unexpected –
out of the blue
the sudden rush
and cold prickling
nerve endings
burning
and freezing –
both.

Your kiss
shot
fire and
ice
through my
feminine
depths

and made me
afraid
and
alive
and aware
of such
wanting.

I am aglow
but afraid
to trust.
Yet I want to
float
and fly
swim and
glide
with this glorious
dangerous
golden
fiery
river

and at last
find
peace.

WHY?

Why do children
need us so much
when young
and then they grow
with our help
they spread their
wings
and we are glad to
see them fly.

But slowly they
leave us behind
and one day we
realise
we need them
more than they
need us.

And we have to
learn to grow
with their help
and spread our
wings
and be glad we've
learned to fly.

WRAP

If I had to choose a haven
your arms would keep me warm.
Yours eyes would give me welcome,
your smile would stop the storm.

Your look stay in my memory
and linger through the night,
your voice, so quietly peaceful
sooth my growing fright..

If I had to choose a harbour
to berth my boat of life
in someone's quiet waters
away from doubt and strife.

Then you would be my watchtower,
my rock and solid base
When all around is churning
I'd see your calming face.

Though the distance is between us,
by space and time apart,
I'll keep you in my longing
and wrap you in my heart.

YOUR TOUCH

When you touch me
I know
what it means
to be
truly
alive.

My skin dances
with the
fire that thrills
and fills
all of my need.

Your soft lips kiss.
Your tongue
glides and melts
its way
down to
my soul.

As I think now
of your skin,
the embrace
we shared,
I burn
with life.

JIM

Sometimes
I can be very foolish
Childlike
Naive.

And sometimes
I am a woman grown
an adult
able to make my own choices.

But always
I am
in love with you –
the very way you walk
the way you think
even
the way you sleep.

When you snore
I still love you
and listen to the sound
that is keeping me awake
blessing the fact
that you are here
at all.

And sometimes
in the dark
reaches of the night,
I wonder
what will I become
when you are gone?

You have helped me grow
and watched me
become what I always knew
I could be.

You have made me
whole
a complete person.

You let me take my
fumbling steps
and never let me fall.